QUEENBOROUGH CASTLE

SHEPPEY'S LOST FORTRESS

David T. Hughes

SEASHEPPEY

2007

First published 2007 by SeaSheppey, 61 Marine Parade, Sheerness, Kent, ME12 2BD.

Cover Illustrations
Two oil paintings by Harold Batzer depicting imaginative perspectives of the castle.
Front: 'Impression of Queenborough Castle as it was Built, A.D. 1361-1366.'
Back: 'Queenborough Castle after Restoration about 1560.'

ISBN 978-0-9557240-0-8

Typeset and printed in Great Britain by Jenwood Printers Ltd, UK, Unit 4, Windsor Industrial Estate, New Road, Sheerness, Kent, ME12 1NB
www.jenwoods.co.uk

QUEENBOROUGH CASTLE

The Isle of Sheppey, lying to the southern side of the Thames Estuary, is separated from the Kentish shore by a navigable stretch of water known as the Swale. During the early mediaeval period the island, nine miles long and five miles at its greatest width, remained sparsely peopled. Its small rural population had its greatest concentration around Minster, one of the highest points on the island. Here stood a nunnery which, possessing extensive lands covering much of the western side of the island, was a major provider of work for the Islanders. A handful of manors lay within Sheppey, the most prominent two of which, Shurland and Norwood, stood in the eastern part of the island. The few hamlets on the island included Bynne, a small community of fishermen's families, no more than some half dozen humble dwellings, situated on the northern flank of a short creek at the western end of the island at a point where the Swale widened out to form a natural harbour and anchorage.

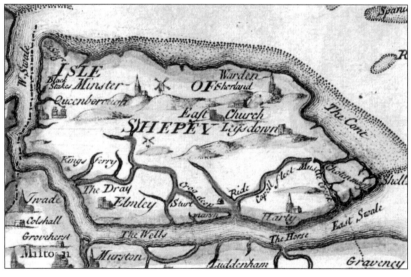

An Early Map of the Isle of Sheppey

Plans for the construction of a castle in Sheppey began in the middle of the fourteenth century during an era when England was in an almost perpetual state of war with one or more of her European neighbours. When the optimistically termed Great Peace was concluded in 1360 between the French and King Edward III of England the two countries had been at continuous war since 1336. Few, however, believed that more than a breathing space had been achieved and Edward took the opportunity

1.

presented by the pause in hostilities to review the effectiveness of his coastal defences. The Isle of Sheppey was found to be especially vulnerable. An enemy that gained control of the island had not only acquired a secure base from which to mount a major attack against mainland Kent, but also mastery over the Swale, an intrinsic part of the important sea route between London and the Continental ports. In spite of this danger the island had been left bereft of any fortification that might protect it or its population in the event of a hostile invasion. With this concern in mind Edward, whose had personal knowledge of the island, and was recorded as having stayed with his friend Sir Walter Manny 'at Russyngdon in Shepeye' in March 1352, gave order by a

King Edward III
From an Effigy at Lincoln Cathedral

Royal Letter Patent of the 10th May 1361, that upon Sheppey a castle should be 'builded for the Strength of his Realme, and the refuge of the inhabitants of the Island.'

The King dispatched Commissioners to Sheppey to survey the island and select the most effective strategic setting for the intended castle. It became apparent that such a fortress might be most advantageously set at the more sheltered western end of the island. Attention focused on Bynne, with its conveniently placed adjacent creek and harbour, and Bynne it would be that was the final choice of site for the erection of the castle. The decision having been made, preparation for embarking upon the building work commenced in August 1361 with the

William of Wykeham
Clerk of Works during the initial building phase of the Castle. A Stone Effigy in the Chapel of Winchester College

purchase from Sir Walter Manny of the manor of Rushenden within which Bynne lay. William of Wykeham, the King's Surveyor and Clerk of Works, and afterwards Bishop of Winchester, was charged with the responsibility of putting in hand the construction. Wykeham was an able man of already proven ability whose previous building projects included major work on the castle at Windsor. Upon his shoulders now rested the many problems associated with assembling in Sheppey the necessary men and materials for the task ahead. Since the island was almost totally devoid of suitable building materials the major part of these had to be imported. Stone was transported from near and far, from quarries in the Medway valley and from places more remote. Much of the stone came from the north of England.

On the 21st June 1361 the King, at Windsor, appointed stonemason Richard de Thwayt 'to select hewers of stone, quarrymen, diggers and other workmen to cut dig and clean the stone which the King has ordained to be purveyed in the quarries of Stapleton and La Roche, co. York, and put them in the quarries to work at the King's wages as long as shall be necessary, to take land and water carriage to bring the stone to his castle of Haddele and the castle which he has begun to build in the Isle of Shepeye, and to imprison all those found rebellious or contrariant in this until he give order touching their punishment.'

The stone, like most of the materials required for the castle, was conveyed to Sheppey by sea, the ships putting into the nearby creek where a wharf had been constructed to allow them to offload their cargoes into waiting carts.

A Ship Unloads Building Materials for the Castle

Timber also presented problems, the majority being acquired from the royal forests, and supplemented by that available locally in Sheppey from the estate of Sir John de Northwode of Norwood manor. A significant quantity of other materials was conveyed over the Swale from the mainland using a crossing place known as Tremmod Ferry (afterwards known as King's Ferry). On each side of the ferry an ancient trackway meandered its way across the marshlands picking out the firmer ground. This track, a mere four feet wide, was substantially widened and improved in order to facilitate the transportation along it of large loads bound for the construction works, it being 'made of a breadth of thirty feet' by decree of Edward, 'for the carriage of carts.' In 1367 mason John Rokesacre received a contract for erecting a 'house for the janitor at the ferry.'

The small army of men needed to build the castle contained few Islanders. Qualified craftsmen such as the stone-masons, carpenters and sawyers had to be summoned from elsewhere. Only for less skilled tasks, such as those of the hauliers and labourers, could island men, with no previous experience of major building projects be used. For Royal works impressment was the customary method of assembling a workforce, imprisonment being the main alternative offered to those who refused. So heavy handed would be the enforced recruitment of the workforce for the building of the castle that on 24th October 1362 a commission of oyer and terminer was appointed to investigate the 'oppressions of the people of the counties of Kent and Sussex by John Stouk and other ministers and purveyors for the works of the King's castle of Shepeye.'

The design for the castle was almost certainly the work of John Box, the master mason who had been given responsibility for on-site supervision of construction and was granted 1s. a day for his services. Under him worked the subordinate masons, or 'hewers of stone,' men like John Rok, Richard Gosling and John Suchlyinge, each of whom received 4d. a day. The carpenters and craftsmen of other trades were paid 3d.

Other names have sometimes been put forward as being responsible for the design of the castle including Henry Yevele who at a later date rose to be the foremost architect or 'devisor of masonry' in the King's service. If Yevele had indeed been the architect it is likely he would have featured prominently in the many surviving rolls and accounts for the building of the castle, but he gets scarce a mention. Edward Gibbon, author of the classic work *Decline and Fall of the Roman Empire* has claimed the distinction for one of his own ancestors, stating in his *Memoirs of My Life* that 'John Gibbon is recorded as the *Marmorarius* or Architect of King Edward the Third; the strong and stately castle of Queenborough which guarded the entrance to the Medway was a monument of his skill.' Examination of contemporary records, however, gives no indication of a John Gibbon in respect to Queenborough Castle or any other building project of the time.

A Mediaeval King Consults
With His Master Mason
From a Contemporary Drawing

Two dwellings in the hamlet of Bynne, the homes of Simon Waryn and John Segar, stood on the site of the proposed castle, and were demolished before work was got underway. With the commencement of building it would not be long before the castle began to take shape, its walls slowly rising above the flat surrounding landscape. Construction, however, did not always proceed steadily. The castle was being built at a time when a flurry of other prestigious building projects were also in hand, mainly in the ecclesiastical field, cathedrals and Archbishops' palaces to the fore, but also with town defences and private castles. This situation placed skilled craftsmen at a premium, and such was the shortage that rival builders vied with each other for the artisans' services, offering various inducements to encourage them into their employment. The shortfall in available craftsmen had been exacerbated through the Black Death, the great pestilence which had arrived in England by 1349, sweeping through the country and wiping out well over a third of the population.

The King, having the power to impress men into service for his own building projects, made savage demands upon an already insufficient pool of experts. Often men were required to abandon for several years the work upon which they were engaged in order to carry out work for the King. Royal monopolization of the best craftsmen led to many disgruntled clients being left in the lurch in mid-construction. These were often driven to offering bribes to craftsmen to persuade them to desert the King's service and return to their original employment. Such was the illegal exodus of Crown workers from Queenborough and other royal sites that, on the 12th March 1362, Edward was obliged to issue to the sheriffs of London an order to 'cause proclamation to be made forbidding any religious person or other master to hire or retain masons or any other craftsmen without the King's command and to take and put them in Neugate prison until further order as for excessive gain and gifts taken by such men for salary and wages in divers parts of the realm contrary to the statute, almost all the masons and craftsmen hired for the King's works in his castles of Wyndesore, Haddeleye and Shepeye have secretly withdrawn, and are retained with religious persons and other masters, to the King's hurt and hinderance of his works, whereat he is moved to anger.'

Besides problems with the labour force the acquisition of necessary materials presented headaches for the builders. Timber was being required in increasingly huge amounts, in addition to the vast quantities of stone, and at one point it was estimated that 689 oaks would be needed. The King grew concerned that, as well as members of his workforce absconding from Bynne, significant amounts of building materials were vanishing. When appointing new clerks to the works at the castle, the stemming of any misappropriation would become a clause in their duties. Thus, for example, when Richard de Blore was engaged on the 13th August 1369, he was expected to investigate 'whether timber, stone and other necessaries bought for the work have been carried away, and have such brought back, and to sell for the King's use the branches and other residues of the trees purveyed for the works'.

In spite of various delays work progressed, and from the Exchequer Accounts it is known that large quantities of candles were transported to the castle so that construction could continue by night as well as day. By 1365 the keep was complete, six bronze vanes being acquired at a cost of 15*s*. each to crown each of its six towers. At the end of 1368 one of the towers also had installed within it a large clock which incorporated a sizeable bell and was one of the earliest known examples to have used a weight driven mechanism. A smaller clock was also provided for the castle chapel. Once the keep was finished attention was directed to completing the rest of the castle and, in 1368, John Box, Maurice Yonge and John Roke were paid £500 for their work in constructing a 55½ perch 1¼ foot section of the outer or curtain wall.

The Building of the Castle Keep

To enable the castle to withstand a long siege it was necessary to make it self-sufficient in its fresh water supply, and large butts were purchased to catch rain water which was then fed into the keep through an elaborate system of lead piping. In practice the system quickly proved to be inadequate. In 1365 Robert de Westmallyng was contracted to dig a 83 feet deep well but it produced little water. The following year he increased the depth of the well by another 12 feet but it still refused to yield sufficient water. It would not be until the year 1393 that the problem of getting fresh water was finally overcome when Robert Weldyker at a fee of 3*s.* 4*d.* a week dug for 60 weeks, employing three masons to line the well with stone until, at a depth of around 200 feet, he broke through the thick layer of clay to the water bearing strata below and water began to fill the well.

By 1368, with the main structure of the castle completed, the time had arrived to pay off the bulk of the workforce and release them from their impressment, for this purpose a warrant being issued appointing Richard de Blore, Richard Cok and William Chaundeler as paymasters. Finishing work was afterwards to carry on for a further two years before the castle became fully operational, its total cost to the King having been over £20,000.

The castle which stood completed in Sheppey had been built on a circular plan and incorporated several novel features. At its centre was placed a massive circular keep, 140 feet in diameter, and with its walls 10 feet thick.

Into the walls of this keep were set six tall circular towers, each projecting for about half its circumference from the walls. To the eastern side of the keep two of the towers were placed closely together to provide defence for the keep entrance which lay between them. Within the keep the apartments forming the domestic and military quarters, and the chapel, were ranged around a circular open courtyard at the middle of which would be sunk the castle well already mentioned.

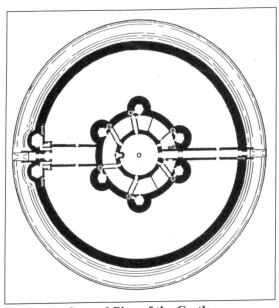

Ground Plan of the Castle
From an Elizabethan Manuscript at Hatfield House

Around the keep was an outer courtyard contained within a concentric curtain wall that was some 1,040 feet in circumference and, outside that, a broad wet moat 60 feet wide and 12 feet deep ringed the castle. The two entrances to the castle were set on opposing sides of the circular curtain wall. The western entrance formed the main gate and was in the form of a twin-towered gatehouse, while the second entrance, set diametrically opposite on the far side of the castle, was a modest though impregnable postern gate. The main entrance was thus situated on the other side to the entrance to the keep, a deliberate ploy to force an enemy who had broken through the main gate to have to work his way in a full half-circle around the keep's walls before he could make an attempt on its entrance. If an enemy managed to negotiate the sturdy curtain wall and gain access to the outer courtyard a pair of parallel walls ran radially inwards from each gateway to the walls of the keep forming two defensive passageways. Halfway along each wall was an entrance to the outer courtyard which could be defended against attackers outside. If, conversely, the enemy was to rush the gateway it was possible for the defenders to contain their attackers within the passageway, denying them access to the outer courtyard.

Much of the finishing work on the castle had been directed towards making the place fit for occupation by the officers and men to be stationed there. Naturally particular attention was paid to the royal apartments. The walls of all chambers that were to be used for accommodation or domestic purposes were plastered and whitewashed, and provided with the necessary furniture and household equipment. Large quanitities of glazing were required for the windows. Externally a fish pond was dug and a garden laid out within the castle grounds, in 1368 Fulk de Peyforer, who had succeeded Wykeham as Clerk of Works, purchasing the seeds for planting in the latter. An early facility provided for the castle had been a watermill, constructed during 1362 adjacent to the wharf used for unloading ships at the nearby creek.

As the castle approached its completion armaments for its protection were brought down by sea from the Tower of London including, on the 12th June 1365, two of the new 'grete' guns along with nine smaller bronze ones that were probably bombards. Guns were then a recent innovation in warfare and Queenborough can claim to have been the first English castle to have been designed with an eye to this new form of weapon, containing several features in common with the later generation of artillery castles built at Deal, Sandown and Walmer by Henry VIII.

Notwithstanding this, it was the well tried and tested traditional types of artillery that Edward III initially turned to provide the main ballistic weaponry for the defence of the castle. Hugh Herland, 'one of the King's carpenters', and others of his trade were employed on site to construct the various 'engines' of war. From 1364 an 'artillour' was placed on the payroll of the castle to have charge of all the weaponry being installed. Among the weapons named at Queenborough in the Exchequer Accounts the most destructive was the trebuchet. First introduced in the late thirteenth century, this device consisted of a long spar, pivoted at around a third of its length so that it could swing in the vertical plane. It worked by counterweight, in its common form weights being hung from the outer end of the shorter arm. At the other end of the spar would be a sling or cradle into which the projectile would be secured. Stone balls were the usual projectile, but the machines were occasionally used to hurl incendaries, and, in the hopes of spreading disease, even dead horses. When triggered the sling-shot effect of the rotating spar would launch its load towards the enemy. Adjustment of the position of the weights on the spar, relative to its pivotal point, allowed a shot to be placed with some accuracy. When Edward was at Queenborough in September 1373 he inspected the weapons that had been installed and was given a special demonstration firing of the trebuchets.

Although being used at Queenborough in a defensive role the trebuchet was fundamentally a seige weapon capable of demolishing the walls of a fortress. Of the weapons assembled at the castle, the springalds, which were specifically designed to be an anti-personnel weapon, were likely to prove most effective in repulsing any enemy. The springald was essentially a giant crossbow which was able to fire a large bolt to highly lethal effect. The bolts were generally made of iron and feathered with wood. When released, such was the kinetic energy imparted to the bolt that it was quite capable of skewering several of the enemy at once if they happened to be standing in alignment.

On the 1st October 1365 Edward appointed Sir John de Foxle as the Constable, or custodian, of the castle, 'he taking at the exchequer £20 yearly for his fee in that office.' Sir John was a seasoned war veteran whose family had long been loyal servants of the Crown, and whose father Sir Thomas Foxle had held the prestigious constableship of Windsor Castle.

Sir John de Foxle
The First Constable
His Memorial Brass in St. Michael's Church Bray-on-Thames

The resumption of the war with France in 1369 caused the castle to be placed in a permanent state of warlike readiness to repel an attack. Expectation of an attempt by the enemy became heightened in 1372 when a large English war fleet was decimated by Spanish allies of the French, leaving Sheppey dangerously vulnerable to a seaborne invasion. By now the English were suffering a number of reversals of fortune on the Continent, the situation moving progressively from bad to worse with the effect that, back on Sheppey, a blow against the castle by the emboldened French became increasingly regarded as likely. In 1374 a large shipment of gunpowder was received from the Tower of London to ensure that the castle's magazines were adequately stocked for its defence. John Arblaster was put in charge of weaponry as Yeoman of Artillery at Queenborough. Throughout the following months the defenders remained on high alert, watching and waiting for the French to put in an appearance.

On the 25th May 1376 Thomas Caterton was delivered up as a prisoner to Foxle at Queenborough under suspicion of having on the 3rd July 1375, in return for a bribe, capitulated the English held castle of Saint Sauveur in France to the enemy. His chief accuser was Sir John Annesley, a man with a vested interest in the French castle, the lordship of which he had expected to gain through his wife Isobel. Within a few days Caterton had been released on bail and the charges against him were not pursued. Annesley, still smarting at the loss of the castle, continued to hold a grudge against Caterton, however, and a few years later, on the 7th June 1380, his animosity resulted in the two fighting a duel before a large crowd of spectators. Annesley would prove the winner, Caterton dying from exhaustion.

In 1377 the French finally delivered their anticipated attack, but not to descend on Sheppey, electing instead to land on a poorly defended stretch of the English coast near Rottingdean. Marching inland they slaughtered a hastily assembled force that hurried to meet them, and razed a large area of the countryside before returning to their ships laiden with loot.

During its construction King Edward had always taken a keen interest in the castle he was causing to be built in Sheppey, in 1363 and on subsequent other occasions visiting the site personally to see how the work was progressing. It would appear that he became somewhat enamoured with the island and, wishing to encourage its development and prosperity, directed that under the protecting walls of his fortress a whole new town should also be established. It was regarded as highly desirable that there should be a local community adjacent to the castle containing the merchants and townspeople needed to provide the everyday services and supplies that it would require. A thriving port upon Sheppey was also seen to be of general benefit to an island that was currently lacking any town or commercial centre.

In January 1324 Edward had married Philippa of Hainault a 'full noble and good woman' who had rapidly achieved great affection from her husband's subjects through her readiness, when necessary, to speak out on their behalf. Not for many years had the realm been served by such a popular Queen. A contemporary chronicler was reflecting generally held opinion when he recorded that 'since the days of Queen Guinevere, who was wife to King

Queen Philippa
From Her Effigy in
Westminster Abbey

Arthur and Queen of England (which men called Great Britain in those days), so good a Queen never came to that land, nor any who had so much honour, or such fair offspring …. Tall and straight she was; wise, gladsome, humble, devout, free-handed, and courteous; and in her time she was richly adorned with all noble virtues, and well beloved of God and Man.' As a tribute, and out of the affection that he bore to his consort, Edward now gave decree that his new town on Sheppey would be known by the name of *Regina Burgus* or, in the English language, the Queen's Borough, soon to become known to all as Queenborough.

For the laying out of the new town, and to allow for its subsequent expansion, much land had had to be acquired from the local landowners; from Sir Walter Manny a tract which lay within the boundaries of the manor of Rushenden, an adjacent tract in the hands of the Savage family, and land that belonged to the nunnery at Minster, all of this ground lying within the flat open area of the island known as Minster Marshes.

Since preparing the site for a town gave no guarantee that men would flock to live there Edward decided that a few inducements were necessary to persuade merchants and other people of substance to set up home. Thus it was that, in issuing the Charter of Incorporation of the town in 1368, the King, in the words of the old historian William Lambarde, created Queenborough 'a free Borough, and made the Townsmen Burgesses, giving them power to choose yeerely a Maior and two Bailifes, that should make their oath of allegeance before the Constable of the Castle, endowing them with Counsance of pleas, with the liberty of two markets weekely, and two Faires yeerely, and benefiting them with freedome of Tholle, and sundrie other bountifull privileges, that might allure men to inhabite the place.'

At the same time Edward, for additional encouragement to the growth of the town, also appointed Queenborough a staple for wool. Thus, along the whole coast between Gravesend and Winchelsea, Queenborough became the sole port through which by law exports of wool had to be channelled, an arrangement convenient to the government, since centralization allowed taxes to be more exactly calculated and collected, and of great advantage to the town because of the increase of trade it necessarily produced. The tax on exported wool was 3d. in the pound. The first Customer (Customs Officer) to be appointed at Queenborough was John Barler, Parson of Wormshill, on the 25th July 1368.

To cater for the religious needs of the expected influx of new citizens to Queenborough the building of a church was begun in 1366 and completed in the next year. The mason responsible was John Rokesacre who, prior to that time, had been working on the construction of the gatehouse and curtain wall of the castle. The stonework and iron grilles for the windows were provided by Thomas Crompe and Stephen-at-Towre respectively. Robert Scotland did the plastering. This building, constructed in the Gothic style, still adorns the town today. Its tower was added at a later period. The bequest of 6s. 8d. in his will of 1481 by John Stanforte, a burgess of the town, for the church 'to the work of the tower' may indicate the date.

Queenborough Church
Was built at the same time as the Castle to serve the new town

In 1369 Queen Philippa died. Much loved by Edward, after her death the King's enthusiasm for the town that he had named in her honour waned and, within a year, he had removed the wool staple to Sandwich. Queenborough

Edward III
In His Latter Years

was afterwards never to achieve the high expectations originally expected of it, remaining for centuries a town of few houses and small population, though never relinquishing the divers rights bestowed on it at its corporation. So it was that Daniel Defoe, having visited the town, wrote in 1724 that he had found it to be 'a miserable, dirty, decay'd, poor, pitiful, fishing town; yet vested with corporation priviledges, has a mayor, alderman, &c. and his worship the mayor has his mace carry'd before him to church, and attended in as much state and ceremony as the mayor of a town twenty times as good.' In the years following Philippa's demise the popularity of Edward began to fade, the rapid deterioration of rule that marked his latter years following hard on her death. Although his interest in the town had diminished Edward continued on occasion to take up residence in his castle at Queenborough. In the National Archive at Kew are held numerous Ordinances and Letters Patent, dated from Queenborough, that were issued by the King during his various stays at the castle. Edward finally died on the 21st June 1377 after a reign that had spanned fifty years. Until almost the end of the reign of Edward III the keepership of the castle had remained in the hands of the stalwart old campaigner, Sir John de Foxle. However on the 5th October 1376 it was transferred into the hands of the King's son, the 37 years old John of Gaunt, with Sir John de Foxle being given instead the custodianship of the castle at Southampton. De Foxle's tenure of his new post was to prove to be of fairly short duration for in December 1378 he died, his body being conveyed to the family chapel at St. Michael's Church, Bray-on-Thames, and buried between those of his first and second wives. At Edward's death, his eldest son Edward (the Black Prince) having predeceased him, the throne of England was passed to his grandson as Richard II.

On the 9th December 1381 John of Gaunt farmed out the constableship of the castle to John Kent. During Kent's tenure of the office a tower of the castle was seriously damaged and other parts of the fortress suffered lesser damage when, on the 21st May 1382 a violent earthquake rocked the island. Considerable exchequer funds were expended to rectify the damage. The well in the central courtyard was blocked and required clearing and repair of its shaft.

John of Gaunt
The second constable of the Castle

There would be a new Castellan in 1384 when, on the 28th October of that year Thomas Atte Lee was granted the post for life at a fee of £10 a year. On the 17th January 1385 there was made a 'Grant to the King's esquire Thomas atte Lee, Constable of Quenesburg Castle, that during the war he have two yeomen therein for its safe custody receiving 3d. daily for each at the hands of the Sheriff of Essex.' With a few months, however, he was required to vacate the post when, on the 13th March 1385, at the behest of Richard, he was succeeded by Robert de Vere, Marquis of Dublin and Earl of Oxford.

Robert de Vere was the chief favourite of the King and held extraordinary influence over him which aroused the jealousy of the other nobles to open expression. Such was the hostility regarding de Vere's relationship to the King that, in bestowing upon him the castle at Queenborough Richard found it necessary to invoke 'the curse of God and St. Edward and the King' upon all who should do or attempt anything against the grant. While he was in office at Queenborough further repair was

Richard II
The young King whose Intimate Friendship with the Constable of Queenborough would bring chaos to the Country.

15.

carried out on the castle, by Letters Patent of the 16th May 1385 John Lancastre, Robert Potter, chaplain, Richard Cherstoke and John Hunt being appointed 'to take sufficient masons, carpenters and labourers in Kent, except in the fee of the church, for the repair of the Earl of Oxford's castle of Quenesburgh and set them to work at the said Earl's charges, with power to imprison the disobedient.'

Eventually, in 1387, the nobles entered into open conflict with de Vere, defeating him and his confederates at Radcot Bridge. Reaching London safely disguised as a groom de Vere, after a hasty interview with the King, fled down to his castle in Sheppey. From Queenborough the castle's now fugitive Constable took ship to the Low Countries, and from thence into exile in Louvain where he was to remain until his death following a hunting accident in 1392.

De Vere's flight to the Continent having left the constableship of Queenborough vacant, the post was granted to Sir Digory Seys, a mandate being issued on the 27th December 1387 'to all inhabiting the castle of Quenesburgh in the county of Kent, and holding the same, to deliver it with all its victuals and artillery to the King's knight, Diggory Seys, appointed to keep the same to the King's use, an indenture being made between him and the principal occupier of the castle, for which due allowance shall be made.'

By a missive dated the 13th January 1388 the new constable was ordered 'to suffer John Lopham sergeant at arms, John Boys and William Benyngton esquires, whom the King is sending with this writ, to order the castle, repair at pleasure to the places where divers goods and chattels of the King's property in gold and silver and other harness are hidden, and to remove them all whatever they be, and bring them to the Council at Westminster, dearresting and delivering to the said William his horses and harness which are there under arrest; as the King and Council have information that such goods are hidden within the castle, and by advice of the Council the King's will is that they be brought to the Council for furtherance of the King's business and the business of the realm.'

On the 4th January 1393 a local knight, Sir Arnold Savage of Bobbing, assumed the Constableship in the stead of Diggory Seys. Savage had been Sheriff of Kent in 1381 and 1385, and received his knighthood in 1385 while on campaign with the King against Scotland. During his term of office he undertook a further series of repairs and improvements to the castle, receiving for the purpose various sums from the Crown totalling around £220. Although, having served for four years in the office, Sir Arnold stood down from the constableship of Queenborough, he continued to hold high office, rising to be appointed Speaker of the House of Commons and serving as a Privy Councillor. After his death on the 29th November 1410 he was buried in his parish church at Bobbing.

Sir Arnold Savage
Appointed Constable in 1393. From his Memorial Brass in Bobbing Church

To fill the post of Constable vacated by Savage, King Richard appointed a prominent northerner, Sir William Scrope, also elevating him, on the 29th September 1397, to the title of Earl of Wiltshire. Under royal favour Scrope was also promoted to several more important positions and, on the 17th

Queenborough Castle at the end of the Fourteenth Century
A Painting by Harold Batzer

17.

September 1398, became Treasurer of England. By this time, however, Richard's arbitary government was leading England towards the state of civil war that would culminate in his dethronement. In July 1399 Henry, Duke of Lancaster, son of John of Gaunt, with the support of many of the nobles, formed an army which marched against the King and forced his abdication. Scrope remained Richard's man to the last, valiantly holding Bristol against Lancaster's superior forces. Shortly forced to capitulate he would be condemned to death for his act of defiance and executed at Bristol on the 29th July 1399.

Sir John Cornwall
Constable of the Castle 1402 - 1409

Lancaster now assumed the throne as Henry IV, first of the Lancastrian kings. One of his earliest acts, on the 18th October 1399, was to place the constableship of Queenborough in the hands of a trusted knight, Sir Hugh de Waterton. Three years later Henry replaced Waterton, on the 14th October 1402 granting his post to Sir John Cornwall who had recently become extremely well placed in the Lancastrian Court having married Elizabeth, Dutchess of Exeter, Henry's widowed sister, and thus become brother-in-law to the King.

In 1406 the King paid a visit to the Castle. He and his Court had abandoned London to avoid a plague that was ravaging the city and travelled down to the shelter of Sheppey. When making their departure Henry and his retinue 'took shipp at Quinborowe, in the Isle of Shepeye, for Hadleigh Castle Essex.'

Queenborough was to see another change of Constable on the 27th April 1409 when Cornwall surrendered his office in favour of another of Henry's ardent supporters, Thomas Arundel, Archbishop of Canterbury. In Richard's reign Arundel had been Chancellor, and then Archbishop of Canterbury, but, on the 20th September 1397, being implicated in a

Archbishop Thomas Arundel
Became Constable of the Castle in 1409

plot against the King, was forced to flee to Rome. In 1399 he returned in support of Henry, retook possession of his see of Canterbury and, when Richard was in Henry's hands, also re-assumed his Chancellorship. It was he who crowned Henry at Westminster on the 13th October 1399. While Constable at Queenborough Arundel received a warrant for £66 13s. 4d. to carry out necessary repairs on the castle.

It appears that Arundel gave up the constableship at Queenborough within a couple of years. A commission was formed early in 1412 to investigate 'all felonies and trespasses committed within the town and liberty' of Queenborough, and one of the members appointed to the commission is given as 'Roger Honyn, Constable of the Castle of Quenesburgh.' This is the only known reference to Honyn in regard to the castle, and he remains a shadowy figure from history.

Henry died on the 20th March 1413, his son taking the throne as Henry V and, only the next day, appointing to Queenborough a loyal comrade in arms, Gilbert de Umfraville. Umfraville, the essential fighting man, proved to be a mainly absentee Constable, taking a prominent part in Henry's French wars. He attended the campaign of 1415 at the head of twenty men-at-arms and ninety horse archers and, when on the 22nd September formal surrender was made by the French of Harfleur, stood at the King's right hand bearing the royal helmet and crown. When, shortly afterwards, the English army, though decimated by dysentry, marched northwards, Umfraville shared with the former Constable of Queenborough, Sir John Cornwall, command of the advance guard and it was he who, on the 19th October, first effected the dangerous crossing of the Somme. On the 25th October the English found a large French army barring their way near Agincourt. Thus began the famous battle, Umfraville fighting valiantly to the fore. Agincourt was to prove to be one of the greatest triumphs of English warfare. In an action which lasted barely three hours a depleted and exhausted English force of some five thousand routed an army four or five times its size while losing no more than a hundred men to the perhaps ten thousand dead of the French.

When Henry invaded Normandy in 1417 Unfraville was again in battle, the captain of fifty-four lancers and 125 archers, for the loyal services rendered in this campaign being rewarded with very liberal grants of forfeited Norman estates, including Amfreville, the ancient seat of his family. In January 1421 he was made Marshal of France, in this rôle accompanying the King's son, Thomas, Duke of Clarence, on an expedition against Anjou and its allies. Against Umfraville's expert advice Clarence was unwise enough to attempt a surprise attack on the enemy army by leaving behind his archers and advancing with only men-at-arms to Beauge. There, on the 22nd March, the English suffered total defeat. By the end of the day Clarence had been slain, and the Constable of Queenborough likewise lay dead on the field of battle. Within a few months Henry V was also dead in France, a victim of dysentry, leaving the crown of England to his baby son.

Because Henry VI was only nine months old when he succeeded to the throne the governance of England was placed in the hands of a Protector, John, Duke of Bedford, who remained mainly absent conducting the wars in France. The chief power in the country therefore in reality lay in the hands of two men, Humphrey, Duke of Gloucester, who became the king's Chief Councellor, and Henry Beaufort, Bishop of Winchester. Between these two there was continuous emnity. Bedford died in France in 1435 and was succeeded there by Richard, Duke of York. As the French wars continued there appeared two parties in England; Beaufort's, which included most of the Royal Court, wishful of peace, and Gloucester's, with the young nobles and professional soldiers who took the opposite view.

Early in 1446 the Court party, which held the major influence over the King, decided to strike a blow against its opponents by having Gloucester and some of his chief supporters arrested on charges of treason. Amongst those selected to be apprehended was Sir Roger Chamberlayne who, under the patronage of Gloucester, had been granted the constableship of Queenborough Castle in 1441, the appointment confirmed the 25th January 1542 on the patent rolls. On the 18th February 1446 Royal officers arrived and arrested Chamberlayne and others of Gloucester's associates. Five days later Gloucester himself was found dead, improbably of natural causes. Indictments were brought against the Constable of Queenborough and his companions on the 8th July, and their trials took place in the Court of the King's Bench the following week. The charges were so patently false, however, that the King ordered Sir Roger and the others to be pardoned. At Gloucester's death the leader of the opposition became Richard, Duke of York, who, Henry as yet without children, also became heir-apparent to the throne.

Meanwhile the outlook was becoming very serious in France, with province after province lost until, in 1450, Calais alone remained in English hands. At home the heavy drain of men and money caused by the war was beginning to tell, and the authority of the King proving so weak that anarchy and disorder existed throughout the land. Discontent mounted amongst a population suffering from unjust taxation and monumental corruption by regional officials. In Kent two men were regarded with particular loathing by the many who had become victims of their cruel extortions and oppressions. The first was Sir James Fiennes, created Lord Saye and Sele in 1447, Speaker in the Parliament of 1449, Lord Chamberlain and Treasurer of England; owner by royal decree of a rich mansion at Witley, as well as the great house at Knowle, and of Sayes Court on the Isle of Harty. The other was William Crowmer, Sheriff of Kent, who held the manor of Tunstall in Kent, plus Borstal Hall on the Isle of Sheppey, and was the son-in-law of Saye.

Control of the Channel had by now been torn away from the English, off the southern coasts of England a free-for-all existing, the waters infested by predatory raiders of several nations whose acts of piracy made no merchantman safe. Action against the French at sea was now generally confined to the freebooting activities of a number of private individuals who went out sporadically on their own initiative to hunt down and capture any vulnerable French ship. These private enterprises were motivated mostly by the promise of booty rather than a sense of patriotic duty. For the Queenborough seamen returning to port from such ventures matters were to turn quickly very sour. They discovered that they were not to be allowed to keep their plunder, the majority of which was seized by local government officials and sold, the money thus accrued being used not to reward the seamen, or to compensate the Queenborough merchants whose trade had suffered at the hands of the French, but to line the pockets of the despised Lord Saye. Yet, in spite of this, the sailors continued to prey on French shipping and, by 1450, Queenborough has become a veritable nest of pirates.

In April 1450 some French raiders stormed boldly into Queenborough harbour and wreaked havoc, only the daunting presence of the castle and its garrison preventing them from causing worse damage ashore, while the town of Harwich on the Essex coast, sacked by enemy night-raiders, had cause to regret that it did not likewise enjoy the protection of a castle. These audacious raids were to some extent by nature of a reprisal; the French striking at the known bases of those who were inflicting the most damaging attacks on their shipping.

Queenborough was now a seething mass of disaffection, the seamen dismayed at being cheated of their prizes by grasping local officials, and the merchants equally disgruntled because their business was being so disastrously hit. Trade was being strangled because the ships they sent out were never safe, while at the same time friendly foreign traders were reluctant to venture into lawless English waters. As a trading port Queenborough was facing ruin, and the blame was laid squarely upon government ineptitude and corruption.

Jack Cade riding victoriously through the streets of London

General unrest throughout Kent eventually led, at the end of May 1450, to a rising in the county under Jack Cade, a man of mysterious background who used the name John Mortymer and claimed kinship to the Duke of York. On the 31st May the insurgents assembled at Blackheath until they numbered well over 10,000 men. Amongst them was a strong contingent from Queenborough and other parts of Sheppey led by 'John Cheyne of Estchirche in the Isle of Shephey.' Sir John had sat as Member of Parliament for Kent in 1449 and had seen at first hand many of the injustices that prevailed in the county. A valiant knight who had fought at Agincourt, he was also a man well connected, being an uncle by marriage to Margaret Beaufort, Duchess of Richmond, the great grand-daughter of John of Gaunt. His decision to join the revolt could not have been taken lightly, and indicates the depth of feeling that existed at the time. Other Islanders whose names have survived as having supported Cade include John Symond of Mynstre, husbandman, John Swalman of Queneburgh, yeoman; William Baker of Queneburgh, baker; William Britte, John Britte, John Masyn, William Canon, Alan Jacob, Geoffrey Benet, Robert Somter and John Willys, each a 'maryner of Queneburgh.' The most interesting of Cade's supporters from Queenborough was 'John Cokeram, Maior of the Ville of Queneburgh, marchaunt.' The name is probably a scribal error and should read 'Cokerall,' that of a family flourishing in the town at that time.

At Blackheath the Kentishmen presented the King's representatives with a petition entitled 'Bill of Complaints and Requests of the Commons of Kent' which drew attention to the great injustices being suffered by the people of the county. Having received no satisfaction to their pleas Cade and his men eventually crossed London Bridge and occupied the city on the 3rd July. The King had fled the capital but the next day the hated Lord Saye and his reviled son-in-law William Crowmer fell into the hands of the insurgents and were summarily beheaded. The heads of the two executed men, having been carried through the streets of the city on long poles and 'made to kiss one another at the Corners of Eminent Places, to excite laughter from the mob,' were finally set up on their poles on London Bridge.

That evening the people of London belatedly organised their resistance to the unwelcome visitors, and throughout the night a bloody battle raged upon London Bridge with both sides receiving heavy casualties but with no clear victor. The King now saw his chance to end the revolt and, on the 7th July, issued a Royal Pardon to all those who would lay down their arms and return to their homes. This was an astute move. Many of Cade's men had been shocked by the carnage witnessed on London Bridge and, disillusioned with the conduct of their cause, were now ready to accept the King's offer. Soon the bulk of Cade's army was disintegrating, men making their way home in their thousands along the highways and byways of Kent.

Two days after the granting of the pardons Cade, with the still loyal hardcore of his diminished army, arrived in Rochester. By now they had had chance to reflect on the situation, and there were grave doubts as to whether the pardons would be honoured once the King had retightened his grip upon the county, especially in the cases of those who had been most actively involved in the organisation and leadership of the rising. Obviously, their numbers decimated by those who had abandoned the cause, it was no longer viable to make a stand against the Royal forces that it was feared would soon be advancing into Kent. The only alternative lay in flight to safety abroad. Cade examined the options and concluded that the best plan of escape would be to evacuate his little army to the Isle of Sheppey where he believed he would receive a friendly welcome and, with the ferry and Queenborough Castle in his hands, could secure a sufficient breathing space to negotiate for the vessels required to carry himself and his men off to a safe haven overseas.

On the 11th July Cade crossed to the Island with his rump of diehard followers and arrived before the gate of Queenborough Castle. But then came a serious setback to his plans. The Keeper of the castle, Sir Roger Chamberlayne, although always in sympathy with Cade's cause, was also well aware of the course events had taken and the reversal of the rebel leader's fortunes. The man now waiting anxiously beyond the gate was on the run and there could be no future gained by showing him support. Chamberlayne therefore refused to the insurgents access to his castle. Cade, driven to desperation, determined that, having being denied the voluntary surrender of the fortress, he would take it by force and launched his remanent forces in a reckless attack against its walls.

Although Chamberlayne is said to have had a mere two men-at-arms at his disposal the castle, with its cleverly designed defences, proved to be more than a match for the untrained attackers. The assault was a complete failure. Cade, with no experience of storming a defended fortress had, by the end of the day, achieved nothing except the loss of several of his men, including two of his ablest officers, 'Capitaignes' Boucher and Geoffrey Kechyn, both of whom had been taken prisoner. A long siege was out of the question since within a short time the powerful avenging army of Henry VI would be upon them. Flight alone remained for the erstwhile attackers.

The remnants of the once great rebel army dispersed from Sheppey; now it was every man for himself. Cade, travelling light, headed southwards across Kent and 'disguised in strange attire, he privily fled into the wood country.' Soon a troop of the king's men led by Sir Alexander Iden, newly elevated to Sheriff of Kent in replacement of the executed Crowmer, were in hot pursuit finally overtaking 'that great traitor and rebel, who called himself John Mortymer, at Hefeld.' In the short struggle that ensued Cade became wounded 'unto the dethe, and take and carried in a cart toward Londoun, and be the way deide.' At London his body was quartered in the usual manner prescribed for traitors, and his head impaled upon London Bridge whereon so recently had been displayed the heads of Saye and Crowmer.

Iden was to receive 1,000 marks reward for his capture of Cade and was shortly made Constable of Rochester Castle. Soon he would marry

Elizabeth, the widow of Crowmer and daughter of Lord Saye. Sir Roger Chamberlayne was rewarded with 40 marks for his capture of Kechyn and Boucher but, perhaps because of his suspected earlier sympathies for the rebels, was removed from his post at Queenborough Castle. The constableship was then conferred upon Sir Humphrey Stafford, Duke of Buckingham, one of the King's Commissioners sitting at Rochester for the trials of Cade's supporters. These were to be dealt with without mercy, sentences being meted out of such severity that, in the words of one contemporary chronicler, 'men calle hyt in Kente the harveste of hedys.' For his part in this butchery Stafford was not to be forgiven or forgotten by the people of Kent.

John de Northwode, who had served Henry VI as Escheator in Kent, was to be next Constable at Queenborough, receiving a grant of the office on the 4th July 1452, together with the adjacent watermill and a nearby oysterbed known as the 'Kyngs Shelp.' Unusually for one so appointed he was not simultaneously awarded the stewardship of Middelton (Milton).

Sir John Cheyne of Eastchurch, who had actively supported Cade, would afterwards have his pardon of the 7th July 1450 confirmed. His connection with the Beauchamp family must have been of significant help in securing him from some kind of retribution and, of all the knights that followed Cade, he was the only one to be pardoned. His past errors were certainly quickly forgiven for, in February 1452, he was appointed Victualler of Calais, and in 1455 was to replace Iden as Sheriff of Kent. When, in 1457, it again seemed that an invasion by the French was imminent, and a Commander of the greatest reliability was sought for the garrison of Queenborough Castle, it was Sir John Cheyne who was installed there on the 4th February 1458, with a suite of rooms prepared so that he could remain in permanent residence ready to repel any attempt by the enemy.

By this time Henry VI was revealing the signs of an acute mental disorder and lapsing into long periods of insanity. Discontent throughout his realm became more and more openly expressed, and supporters of the powerful House of York began to actively plot against the ruling House of the Lancastrians. The first clash in the Yorkist attempt against the throne came at St. Albans in 1455, resulting in a defeat for the King's forces. Henry then made peace with his opponents, but the old antagonisms remained and, when war flared up again, Richard, Duke of York, formally set a claim on the throne by right of his lineal descent from Lionel, son of Edward III. On the 10th July 1460 the forces of Lancaster and York again met in battle at Northampton, the Commander-in-Chief of the King's army being Sir Humphrey Stafford, Duke of Buckingham, the man whom Henry in the wake of Cade's rebellion had appointed Constable of Queenborough Castle. As a result of the battle the Lancastrians were heavily beaten and were forced to withdraw from the field. Behind them they left the body of their Commander, slain by a group of vengeful Kentish men as he fought beside the King's tent.

The next clash between the opposing armies came at Wakefield in December 1460. Here the Yorkists were to lose their leader, for the Duke of York was killed during the fighting. The Yorkists now sought a leader in the Duke of York's nineteen years old son Edward, and it was he who delivered a decisive blow against the Lancastrian forces at Mortimer's Cross in February 1461. Yorkists now controlled most of the country, and their leader was proclaimed King as Edward IV.

By a grant of the 12th December 1461, backdated to the previous 4th of March, Edward, in acknowlegement of the support that John de Northwode had given to the Yorkest cause, re-appointed him for a second term of office as of Constable of Queenborough Castle, the position he had previously held in 1452. This time he additionally received the lordship of the Hundred of Middelton with fees drawn from its issues. On the 24th February 1462 these fees were determined to be, as 'of old time due and accustomed' in the reign of Richard II, 20 marks a year, and the hundred was instructed to pay de Northwode this amount. Substantial work would be carried out on the castle during de Northwode's tenure as Constable, in 1463 the King issuing warrant for £800 to be paid to Thomas Stratton, his Clerk of Works, for the purpose. Having remained in the post for several years, on the 7th May 1468 de Northwode stepped down in favour of the King's youngest brother George, Duke of Clarence, Lord Lieutenant of Ireland.

Unhappily, before little time had progressed, Edward's relationship with his brother began to deteriorate. In June 1469 Clarence conducted the crafty and ambitious Richard Neville, Earl of Warwick, Lord Warden of the Cinque Ports, from Sandwich to Queenborough where the Earl remained at the castle in conference with his host for several days. The following month the two met again in Calais and there, Clarence, acting against his brother's expressed wishes, married the Earl's daughter, Isabella Neville. From this point onwards it was said that the Duke and his father-in-law were continually plotting the King's downfall.

When Edward crossed to Calais in 1475 for an expedition into France he found it expedient to take his untrustworthy brother with him. Before leaving Clarence was to surrender up his constableship of Queenborough and a large number of his properties. A licence of the 2nd May was issued for him to grant 'the castle and lordship of Queneburgh in the Isle of Shepey, the manors and lordships of Middelton and Marden and the hundred of Middelton' and much more besides to Thomas Bourchier, Archbishop of Canterbury, and others.

George, Duke of Clarence
He became Constable in 1468

In the end Edward would find the on-going duplicity of Clarence intolerable and, on the 16th January 1477, had his brother committed to the Tower of London on a charge of high treason. The case was tried by Parliament on the 15th January 1478 and Queenborough's Constable was found to be guilty of the charges levied against him. Sentence of death was then passed and, when asked to choose the manner of his death, Clarence is said to have elected, with some kind of grim humour, to be drowned in a butt of Malmsey wine, the sentence being duly carried out upon the 18th February 1478.

On the 14th November 1482 Anthony Woodville, Lord Rivers, was appointed for life 'as surveyor and chamberlain of the King's hundreds, manors and lordships of Middelton and Merden in the county of Kent, and captain of the King's castle of Quenbourgh.' The constableship was thus placed in a safe pair of hands for the powerful Lord Rivers was Edward IV's brother-in-law and had a long track record of loyal service to the King.

Edward IV died upon the 9th April 1483 leaving two young sons, Edward and Richard. Prince Edward, then twelve years old, was proclaimed King, his uncle Richard, Duke of Gloucester, immediately assuming the role of Protector. At the time of Edward's death Prince Edward had been with Lord Rivers at Ludlow. Lord Rivers rode with his nephew Sir Richard Grey and a small retinue to deliver the Prince to the Duke of Gloucester at Northampton. In an unexpected turn of events both he and Grey were then seized. They were sent off to Yorkshire in close custody and, at Pontefact Castle, were beheaded on the 25th June 1483. In London the young princes found themselves shortly confined to the Tower, and their 'protector' had assumed the crown as Richard III.

Richard III
He was responsible for major repairs
to the Castle in 1484

In March 1484 King Richard appointed Sir Henry Wentworth of Nettlestead in Suffolk to the position of Constable of Queenborough Castle. Sir Henry's tenure of the castle was to prove to be quite short for just four months later he surrendered the post. His replacement was a Kentish knight, Sir Christopher Colyns, who by his grant of the 20th August 1484 received for life, from midsummer last, 'the office of

Sir Christopher Colyns
The Constable in 1484 A print made
in 1806 from an original painting

28.

constable of the King's castle of Quenebugh' along with 'a mill adjoining the castle at 20 marks yearly for the office as Arnold Savage, Knight, constable in the time of Richard II, had from the issues of the counties of Essex and Hartford, with all other profits.' Early in the next year Richard ordered a major programme for modernising and strengthening the castle, to which end he issued warrants, dated the 16th February 1485, for 'timber to be delivered to Christopher Colyns, for certain reparations, at the Castle of Quenesburghe,' and dated the 10th April 1485 giving Colyns authority to 'take masons, stones, and other material necessary for the works in the said Castle.' The renovation of one of the drawbridges would be one of the tasks carried out.

During the early days of Richard's reign a crime was committed which would arouse the people's anger and was eventually to cost him the throne. The two young princes, Edward and his brother Richard, disappeared from the Tower never to be seen again, and were generally believed to have been murdered. Those who opposed the rule of Richard now turned their hopes on Henry Tudor, son of Edmund Tudor and his wife Margaret Beaufort, great grand-daughter of John of Gaunt. On the 1st August 1485 Henry Tudor arrived from France with a large army in support. At his side there rode Sir John Cheyne of Eastchurch in Sheppey, whose grandfather had joined Jack Cade, and who, as a militant supporter of those who rejected Richard's reign, had fled to join Henry in exile. The King's forces marched to meet Henry's and, on the 22nd August 1485, they met at Bosworth Field. The bravest fighter that day was Richard himself. Spurring his horse forwards and hacking his way through his enemies he killed Sir William Brandon who was Henry's standard bearer, unhorsed Sir John Cheyne, and came within an ace of killing Henry personally, only then to be overwhelmed and slain. So came the end of Richard, the last of the Yorkist kings.

Richard's two surviving commanders from the battle, Henry Percy, Earl of Northumberland, and Thomas Howard, Earl of Surrey, were treated with surprising leniency, being escorted as prisoners to Queenborough Castle where they lived in relative comfort until being afterwards released and their estates restored.

Henry Tudor, now to rule England as Henry VII, had acquired with the crown some forty castles, including the Tower of London, Windsor and Queenborough, and it was to be William Cheyne, younger brother of Sir

John Cheyne, that he would select from among his followers to be Constable of the latter. Cheyne held the post for two years until 1487 when, on the 12th May, he was superseded by Sir Anthony Browne of Betchworth, Standard Bearer of England, who had been serving as Constable of Calais, a post which he would still retain.

Henry VII
His seizure of the Throne of England gave him
Possession of Queenborough Castle

Browne remained Constable of Queenborough for over eighteen years. Around 1505 his continuing reliability would become suspect. The King had recently been seriously ill, with the possibility he might die, but had made a recovery. A report then reached his ears of a conversation which had taken place at Calais between Sir Anthony Browne, Sir Hugh Conway and other officials there. Conway had voiced the opinion that they should all be looking to their futures, the King being now 'but a weak and sickly man, not likely to be a long-lived man,' and there being many contenders who might succeed to the throne. It was claimed that Browne then said darkly that he had 'good holds to resort to' which would keep him in good stead 'howsoever the world might turn.' His wife Lucy Neville, a niece of Richard Neville, Earl of Warwick, was a Yorkist who 'loveth not the King's grace,' and it is likely that Browne, keeping his options open, had entered into some secret dialogue with the King's enemies, many of whom were living in exile in France. Browne escaped whatever retribution Henry might have been contemplating for his seemingly disloyalty, perhaps even treachery, by dying on the 25th September 1505.

A new Constable was now required for Queenborough and, on the 12th November 1506, Henry granted the office 'from Michaelmas last' to Sir Francis Cheyne, of the manor of Shurland in Sheppey. He was the eldest son of the former Constable Sir William Cheyne by Isabel, the daughter of Sir William Boleyn.

On the 21st April 1509 came the death of Henry VII, his eighteen years old son then assuming the throne as Henry VIII. Dated the 30th November 1509, one of his first acts specific to Sheppey was to confirm to Sir Francis Cheyne his position as 'Constable and Porter of Quenebourgh Castle.' The tenure of Sir Francis would however be cut short by his premature death on the 20th January 1512 and, on the 4th March 1512, it was his half-brother Sir Thomas Cheyne who succeeded him at Queenborough. Shortly prior to this event Sir Thomas had also been granted the coveted post of Lord Warden of the Cinque Ports. When Henry went to war with France in 1513, Sir Thomas, who had risen rapidly in the King's favour, was entrusted with the position of greatest responsibility as Commander-in-Chief of the armies, being present in this capacity at the siege of Therouenne and the Battle of Guinegaste.

In January 1533 three mariners, possibly the worse for drink, set about and broke up the gate of the castle. They were apprehended and taken before Sir Thomas who sent them to the Mayor to be detained until the 'King's pleasure' was known in the matter. The following night, however, the men somehow escaped and made their way back on board their vessel, an English crayer, or small trading craft, lying in the harbour. The mayor and his bretheren were soon on their trail and, after overcoming some resistance from the master of the vessel, managed to recover the fugitives. Cheyne on being informed of the incident ordered that the master should also be taken into custody and his vessel impounded until further orders. He wrote to the Privy Council on the 16th January stating that the arrested mariners were suffering greatly from the cold in prison, and that he awaited orders what action he should take with them. History, however, does not go on to relate what kind of punishment the men would subsequently receive.

John Multon (or Moulton), King's Master Mason, spent five days in company with the Master Carpenters and Thomas Cunne, Sergeant Plumber, inspecting the castles of Queenborough and Leeds in 1535. The two Master Carpenters who helped view the castles were William Clement and John Russell. The Court of Augmentations was established in 1535 to administer the lands surrendered by the dissolved monasteries. In 1545 Henry, with money that had become available from the monastries, ordered a refurbishment of Queenborough Castle with various modifications being made to its structure to bring it into line with the great strides that were then being made forwards in the use of artillery, the work being carried out, we are told by the Tudor historian William Lambarde, 'at such time as hee raised Blockhouses along the Sea coasts, for the causes already rehearsed in Dele [namely that "having shaken off the intolerable yoke of the Popish tyrannie, and espying that the Emperour was offended for the divorce of Queene Katherine his wife, and that the French King had coupled the Dolphine his sonne to the Popes niece, and maried his daughter to the King of Scots, so that he might more iustly suspect them all, than safely trust any one, determined (by the side of God) to stand upon his

Henry VIII
Converted the castle for use as an Artillery Fortress in 1536

owne gardes and defence: and therefore with all speede, and without sparing any cost, he builded Castles, platfourmes, and blockhouses, in all needefull places of the Realme"].

Of this Castle at Quinborow, Leland saith thus,

> *Castrum Regius editum recipit*
> *Burgus, fulmina dira, & insulanos*
> *Tutos servat, ab impetu vel omni.*
>
> A Castle high, and thundring shot,
> At Quinbroughe is now plaste:
> Which keepeth safe the Ilanders,
> From every spoile and waste.'

One of the blockhouses ordered by Henry was built some two miles distant from the castle at the extreme north-western point of the island where there lay a windswept promontory of marshland known as Sheer Ness. The initial funding for this blockhouse was incorporated in a warrant for £500, given to Sir Richard Lee in May 1545 'for the fortificacion of Quinborough Castle and th'Isles of Sheppy and Grayne.' To the eastern side of the blockhouse two small bulwarks were also shortly erected, suitably spaced in order to protect the vulnerable low-lying section of land that stretched along the coastline until the clay cliffs of north Sheppey began to rise.

In order to supplement the troops defending Sheppey, musters were held during the year in the local mainland hundreds. These raised 126 men to be sent to the island, along with personal hand arms and equipment which were seemingly often deficient (e.g. 'xxv byllemen all lackyng colars, and on a shworde' and 'ij gunners lackyn mattche and powdour'). On the 26th August 1545 a warrant was issued by the Privy Council to the Treasurer and Chamberlains of the Exchequer to deliver £200 to Nicholas Arnold, Captain within the Isle of Sheppey, for the 'entertainment' of himself and the soldiers under his command. Further warrants to Arnold followed; one of the 21st February 1546 giving £240 'for the charges of his owne entreteignement and his retynew at Quynbourough,' and another on the 4th June following, for £200 to be passed into 'thandes of Thomas Crompe, servaunt to Nicholas Arnolde, to be delyvered in prest to his master according to his request by his letters, for charges of the garryson at Quynborough.'

Arnold continued to be issued with sums of money for the upkeep of the garrison until the autumn of 1546 when he was superseded in command by Sir William Woodhouse. The payments to Queenborough continued. On the 14th November the Privy Council authorised a warrant for £38 6s. 10d. 'to the Treasurer of thaugmentacions to delyver to Sir William Woodhouse for wages of the garyson at Quynborowe.' By a similar warrant of the 23rd January 1547, he received a further £26 3s. 2d. 'to be

Old Oak Muniment Chest
Claimed to have once belonged to the Castle

by hym paid over to the souldiours within the Castle of Quynburgh, and the iij blokhouses there, for their wages from the vij[th] November last till the xix[th] of this instant.'

In all over £2,000 was advanced for the defence of Sheppey during the latter years of Henry's reign, mainly by warrant from the Court of Augmentations. Cannon were placed in the blockhouse to command the entrance to the Medway and, on the 16th November 1547 the Privy Council granted money specifically for 'viij persons serving in the Castell of Quenesboroo and the Blockhus at Sheenes in thisle of Shepey' so that each might be paid gunners' wages 'after the rate of vjd. by the daye.'

By this time there was a new King, for Henry VIII had died on the 28th January 1547 bringing to the throne his nine-year-old son as Edward VI. Edward was a devout Protestant. Throughout his reign tensions with France and the rest of Catholic Europe remained, with the result that a strong garrison continued to be maintained at Queenborough Castle ready to repulse any surprise attack on Sheppey. At the beginning of 1551 it was decided to replace the blockhouse at the north-western tip of the island with a larger defence. In preparation for this, on the 27th January 1551 the Privy Council issued a 'lettre to Mr. Rogers, of Fustone, to commune with Thomas Cheyney, Threasorer of the Kinges Howseholde, for the situacion and making of a Bulwerke at Sheres Neyshe.'

On the 6th July 1553, Edward, never of robust health, died still aged only fifteen, having reigned six years. This brought his half-sister Mary to the throne, who was an uncompromising Catholic determined to return England to the Church of Rome. Much to the dismay of many of her subjects, including Catholics, in May 1554 Mary married a foreigner, King Philip II of Spain. With her succession the threat of invasion immediately subsided, and there was to be no further outlay expended on strengthening Queenborough Castle and its satellite defences, though it was not until 1557 that the maintainance of a garrison at the castle was finally discontinued.

The death of Mary on the 17th November 1558 brought Queen Elizabeth I to the throne and a return of England to Protestantism which again raised the spectre of invasion, now particularly by Spain. The Privy Council gave immediate consideration to reintroducing a garrison for Queenborough Castle and in December produced a note regarding the allowances that would be required for this. The proposal was not followed up however, so it is apparent that no imminent danger was perceived.

Sir Thomas Cheyne had held the Constableship of Queenborough for almost half a century. A man who must have possessed an amazing flexibility of attitude and conscience, he managed to survive and prosper during all the violent swings of religious and political outlook that occurred within his lifetime. As well as Constable of Queenborough and Lord Warden of the Cinque Ports he was to be made a Knight of the Garter, rose to become a Privy Councillor, was appointed Treasurer of the Royal Household, and served as Lord Lieutenant of Kent. Throughout the reign of Henry, and in the succeeding reigns of Edward VI and of Mary, he retained high office, remaining in Royal favour right

Sir Thomas Cheyne
His tomb effigy in the parish church at
Minster in Sheppey

until his death, which occurred on the 8th December 1559, shortly after the accession of Queen Elizabeth. In his will he desired to be buried upon Sheppey, his 'tombe to be made nygh to the place where my late wyef Frydeswith do lye in my chapel at Minster.' His wishes were duly carried out, the burial taking place on the 4th January 1560 in the small family chapel adjoining the north-eastern corner of the parish church. When this chapel was later demolished the tomb of Sir Thomas with its fine alabaster effigy was moved within the walls of the adjacent church where it remains until this day.

Elizabeth, to fill the vacancy left by the death of Sir Thomas, granted the keepership of the castle on the 3rd May to Sir Robert Constable of Everingham in Yorkshire. During Elizabeth's reign the position held an annual salary of £29 2s. 6d. A few months after granting the constableship of Queenborough to Sir Robert, in 1560 Elizabeth paid a visit to her castle. At the beginning of December the Queen, having spent time at Greenwich and Eltham, proceeded down river with her retinue to the Isle of Sheppey. Having been entertained by Sir Robert Constable at Queenborough castle for

a few days, Elizabeth returned up river to London in good time for Christmas. Sir Robert would retain his post as custodian of the castle only until the 21st June 1561 when by assignment he passed it to John Thornton of Milton. The post would again change hands on the 2nd November 1567 when it was re-assigned to Thomas Randolph of Badlesmere.

Queen Elizabeth I
Visited Queenborough and stayed at the Castle in 1560

Queenborough was at this time about to become the home of an interesting piece of commercial enterprise when a small chemical processing plant was established at the castle. Of this venture Lambarde tells us: 'Being at this Castle (in the yeere 1579) I found there, one Mathias Falconar (a Brabander) who did (in a furnesse that he had erected) trie and drawe very good Brimstone and Copperas, out of a certein stone that is gathered in great plenty upon the Shoare neare unto Minster in this Ile.' The copperas stones were washed out of the cliffs by the continuous action of the sea into convenient deposits on the beach where they could be gathered and conveyed to the castle. Brimstone, or sulphur, had a variety of uses, which included use as one of the constituents of gunpowder. Copperas was used in tanning and dyeing, and in the manufacture of ink. The copperas industry in Sheppey was to last until well into the nineteenth century, at its peak thousands of tons of copperas stones being exported annually from the island.

Thomas Randolph died on the 8th June 1590. Queenborough was already effectively under the constableship of Sir Edward Hoby who had been resident in castle since 1582, but it would not be until the 9th July 1597 that he would eventually receive his formal grant of the position. He was vexed not to have received the customary simultaneous grant of the stewardships

An Elizabethan Sketch of the Castle in 1574

of the manor of Milton and the hundred of Milton, which remained with Ursula Copinger, Randolph's widow. After Randolph's death Hoby had, on the 28th January 1592, unsuccessfully petitioned trying to win for himself the stewardships. The castle lay within Milton hundred, which caused Hoby to complain how inconvenient it was 'to be under a woman' and stating that it could 'not be without touche of disgrace, in my time, & especiallie in this time, to have that severed which so manie hundred yeares, both before her lease and after, hath still gon together.'

An able administrator, and a man of considerable learning, Hoby was an intimate of the distinguished Elizabethan historian William Camden who, when writing of the castle, thought it worthy to note: 'The present constable is Sir Edward *Hobey*, my particular friend, who has improved his noble mind by literary studies.' Before his appointment at Queenborough the charismatic Hoby, under the auspices of his uncle Lord Burghley, had risen into high favour at Court, and been frequently entrusted to carry out confidential missions on behalf of the state. Queenborough had the privilege, granted by Elizabeth in 1571, of being represented by two members in Parliament, and, on the 24th September 1586, Hoby was one of those elected by the Borough for return to the House. Here he rapidly gained distinction as being a speaker of note.

In July 1588 Hoby was chosen to investigate and report to Elizabeth on the preparations being made against the Spanish Armada. In Sheppey there were fears that the island might be the intended invasion site and the castle was put on full alert. For the added protection of the island the Privy Council sent a letter on the 8th July to the deputy lieutenants of Kent, ordering 'a sconce to be made within the Isle of Sheppey at a place over against the Kinge's Ferrie,' expressing no doubt that they would 'deale verie effectuallie with th'inhabitantes for the speedie execucion thereof.' When, within the month, the Armada sailed, Hoby was in the English ships that sailed out to meet it and, after the famous victory, he was to take into custody at Queenborough a number of spanish prisoners brought back on ships returning from the conflict to the Nore. One of the more distinguished of his captives, believed to have been the wealthy Jeronimo Magna, died in 1591, whilst still in internment at Queenborough, and was taken to the parish church at Minster for burial. The event was recorded in the Church Register for the 5th December, with the information that he was 'Signior Jeronimo, a Spanyarde Prisoner to Sir Edward Hoby, taken in the Fighte with the Spanishe flete. 1588.'

Although successive Tudor Constables had made improvements to the living accommodation, so that the castle could serve as a comfortable residence as well as a fortress, it was Hoby, more than any of his predecessors, who was responsible for bringing a degree of elegance into the decor and fittings. Amongst various innovations he collected and displayed on the walls of the castle the portraits of the former Constables of the castle, adding to them his own. Under his direction the great dining hall was also decorated in a luxurious style befitting of the holding of sumptuous banquets, with a particularly magnificent ceiling around which were arranged 44 coats of arms of the formost nobility and gentry then living in Kent. In the middle of these was set the coat of arms of Elizabeth herself, with a salutatory inscription in Latin underneath:

> Lilia vergineum pectus regale leonis
> Significant; vivas virgo, regasque leo;
> Umbra placet vultus, vultus quia mentis imago;
> Mentis imago placet, mens quia plena Deo;
> Virgo Deum vita, Regina imitata regendo,
> Viva mihi vivi imago Dei.
> Qui leo de Juda est, et flos de Jesse, leones
> Protegat et flores, Elizabetha, tuos.

> Lillies the lion's virgin breast explain,
> Then live a virgin, and a lion reign.
> Pictures are pleasing, for the mind they shew;
> And in the mind the Deity we view:
> May she who God in life and empire shews,

To me th' eternal Deity disclose!
May Jesse's flower, and Judah's lion deign
Thy flowers and lions to protect, great Queen.

A.D. 1593.

The flowery verses may well represent more than just Hoby's natural admiration for his Queen. He was hopeful of a Royal visit to the castle and was trying to re-ingratiate himself with Elizabeth whose displeasure he had recently incurred. Hoby, distinguished as an orator in Parliament had, since the beginning of his political career, revealed himself to be a man of progressive and often radical views, and it was inevitable that some of his opinions would irritate a few of the older and more conservative members of the House. In 1593, however, a serious clash took place when Sir Edward came into conflict with Sir Thomas Heneage, the Vice

Sir Edward Hoby
from his Effigy on the Hoby Family
Tomb at Bisham

Chancellor and a Privy Councillor. Tempers flared and there was a heated exchange of words. When Heneage afterwards reported the incident to Elizabeth, levying the claim that Hoby had subjected him to a barrage of personal insults, the Queen was furious. She decided to make an example of Hoby for showing disrespect to one of her Privy Councillors, and caused him to be kept in confinement until near to the end of the parliamentary session, which came about on the 10th April 1593. The Queen would afterwards quickly forgive Sir Edward his transgression, and he was thenceforth careful to remain in Royal favour.

In August 1595 Hoby, along with George Carew, was appointed to reorganise the records of the herald's office. Carew had formerly been a sea captain under Sir Humphrey Gilbert, taking place in 1578 in his abortive expedition to the West Indies. In the November following his appointment to the herald's office he would receive grant of the manor of Hadlow in Kent and a moity of the neighbouring manor of Tonbridge, their combined value being £30 10*s*. In the summer of 1596 Carew went on the expedition to Cadiz where, it was afterwards alleged, he stole 44,000 ducats worth of gold from Cadiz Castle. He protested his innocence, claiming to Sir Robert Cecil that he had 'not one piece of coin, any jewel, or more than one piece of plate not worth 50*s*.' With no direct evidence against him the matter was dropped, although the suspicions remained. While returning home to Kent he was detained by toothache at Queenborough Castle. Sir Edward Hoby informed Cecil, 'it showeth what he deserveth if he had his right, and how your honour should use him, the heavens having concluded him worthy of a prison.' Notwithstanding this it appears that the following year Hoby, who had recently been officially appointed Constable of Queenborough, gave support to Carew enabling his election as a representative of Queenborough in Parliament. This was despite Sir Moyle Finch, Sheriff of Kent, darkly warning the borough that if it was 'evill supplied' the Privy Council would 'have occasion to enquier and find out by whose default the same hath happened.'

In 1607 Hoby took the mayor, baliffs and burgesses of Queenborough to law in a case eventually heard before Lord Dorset and Sir Julius Cæsar. He claimed that, as Constable of the castle, all the profits of the lands and tenements in the borough belonged to him as agent for the Crown, and also that Richard II had made a 'chase' of the town. These claims were successfully refuted by the corporation.

Sir Edward Hoby eventually died on the 1st March 1617, while in residence at Queenborough, his body afterwards being conveyed to Bisham in Berkshire, the seat of his family, for burial.

A Stylised Representation of the Castle Keep
On the front dated 1610 in Queenborough Parish Church

Queen Elizabeth had died in 1603, her successor, the first of the Stuart kings, arriving from Scotland to assume the throne as James I. In the early years of the new reign Philip Herbert was acknowledged to be chief of the Royal favourites, sharing with the King a passion for hunting and field sports.

A man of no great intellect, in the words of Clarendon, 'he pretended to no other qualifications than to understand dogs and horses very well.' Such was Herbert's royal standing that when, on the 27th December 1604, he married Susan Vere in an ostentatious ceremony at Whitehall the King himself had taken a prominent part. Herbert had at this time recently begun an intimate association with Sheppey, early in 1604 the King having granted him possession of Shurland Hall, Eastchurch, the former seat of the Cheyne family. On the 4th May 1605 the King created him Baron Herbert of Shurland and, on the same day, Earl of Montgomery. Herbert's ties with the Island became further strengthened when in March 1617 James awarded him the constableship of Queenborough Castle, recently vacant through the death of Edward Hoby. Further elevation followed. On the 17th March 1623 he was created Lord Lieutenant of Kent, on the 3rd August 1626 Lord Chamberlain and, with the death of his brother on the 10th April 1630, became Earl of Pembroke.

In comparison with the literate and sophisticated Sir Edward Hoby Queenborough was now presented with a Constable in an entirely different mould. Philip Herbert, Earl of Montgomery, a man of little refinement, was both bad-tempered and foul-mouthed, with a lust for the most basic pleasures of life. Although he would spend little time in residence at Queenborough he would not be slow to use his position as Constable of the castle in order to advance the interests of his cronies.

Queenborough, still failing abysmally after two and a half centuries to realise the aspirations of Edward III for it to become a thriving town and port, possessed less inhabitants than many a modest village. Since 1571, when the town had first gained the right to elect two Members of Parliament, the number of adult males in its population had continued to hover at around thirty. So small was the electorate that the Mayor and

Philip Herbert, Earl of Pembroke
The Last Constable of the Castle

Corporation were placed in the position of being able to control who was returned to Parliament. They would select who were to represent the town, the subsequent election then being little more than a formality. Whilst always fiercely guarding its rights and privileges, the town generally sought to maintain a good rapport with its most prominent and influential citizen, the serving Constable of the castle. Reflecting this, by the reign of James I the situation had grown whereby the Mayor and Corporation would pick one of the Parliamentary candidates, but gift the choice of the other to the Constable.

As Herbert's constableship progressed he would become increasingly dissatisfied with the existing arrangement concerning the nomination of Members for Parliament. On the 6th November 1620 he had written from London to the 'Mayor and Brethren' stating that 'since it hath beene heeretofore the costome at Quenborough that the Captayne and Porter of the Castell there hath had the nomonation of one Burgis of Parlament at the lest at his disposinge as often as there hath been occasion; now that his maie is pleased to cale a Parlament I doe request at your handes the same privelidg wch formerly my p^edecessors have had.' He went on to nominate one Roger Palmere as his choice, and noted that the town's own choice was 'my servant Frowd at wch I am well pleased.' Having thus had two of his own associates selected to represent the town, Herbert came to believe that in future the same situation should prevail. On the 6th January 1624, with another election pending, he wrote to the Mayor and Jurats of the town thanking them for having 'soe freely conferred one Burgess' place at my disposinge and the other upon Mr Bassett.' But Herbert was not content at having secured one Parliamentary seat for a friend, he wanted *both* places, and he continued in his letter to 'presume upon their love so farr as to make a promise to engage my credit wth you ' for two of his special friends Roger Palmer and Robert Pooley, and 'to give way unto mee for this tyme to nominate these two gents.' Bassett, Herbert claimed, had agreed to stand down 'by reason of other employment.' Presumably some pressure had been brought to bear upon him. So it was that, on the 22nd January 1624, Queenborough's two Parliamentary representatives became Herbert's acolytes Palmer and Pooley.

In the Borough there was by now a fast growing resentment and resistance to the Constable's interference in the town's affairs, and for the Parliament of 1625 the Burgesses nominated a popular local man, Sir Edward Hales, in preference to one of Herbert's choices. The knowledge of this infuriated Herbert and, on the 25th April, he wrote again to the Corporation:

> 'After my hastie commendacions I have just cause to make ye worst construccion of your undiscreete carriage towardes mee in slighting my letters which I directed unto you for Mr Robert Pooley, a gent. every way able to discharge a greater trust than happily might betide him from that Corporation, if you had made choice of him according to the tenor and meaning of my sayd letters. And assure yourselves since Sir Edward Hales out of respect to mee is Content to wave acceptance of that Burgesseshipp wh. yee would enforce upon him, if in his Roome you choose not the sayd Mr Pooley for whom you see how much I am engaged, I shall consider it as a neglect and scorne doubled uppon mee, and shall most assuredly therefore whensoever your occasions shall need my furtherance bee found
>
> Yor. friend according to yor. behavior.
to mee in this and in ye future,
Montgomery.'

The Mayor and Corporation were not to be cowed and on the forthcoming election day, the 9th May 1625, stuck to their original decision, returning Sir Edward Hales with Roger Palmer for the new Parliament.

In March of 1625 James I died bringing his son to the throne as Charles I. Herbert had managed to retain Royal favour throughout the reign of James, being a kindred spirit with the King who continued to bestow various high offices upon his favourite. At the beginning of the new reign Philip Herbert, Earl of Montgomery, found himself still in high standing at Court and, in the first month, was dispatched to Paris with an embassy that was to conduct the Princess Henrietta Maria to England where, in June 1625, she was to marry Charles. It was also Herbert who bore the spurs at Charles's coronation on the 2nd February 1626. Queenborough's Constable, however, was greatly disliked by the new Queen and, as Charles's reign progressed, the Earl's uncouth behaviour and rough manners gradually led to him becoming alienated from the Court. When, on the 23rd July 1641, Charles was eventually moved to dismiss Herbert from his office as Lord Chamberlain, the Constable thenceforth identified himself with the mounting parliamentary opposition to the King.

The storm clouds were by now gathering over England. Since the previous century the House of Commons had progressively widened its effective power to govern the country. The autocratic Charles, on the other hand, believed uncompromisingly in rule by Divide Right, and inevitably came into increasing conflict with Parliament over whose authority should

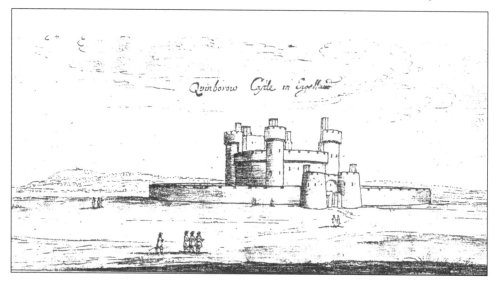

Queenborough Castle as it appeared around 1640
From a drawing by Wenceslas Hollar now held in the British Library

ultimately prevail in the land. Sympathies polarised and in August 1642 civil war broke out between Charles and the forces of Parliament. In the series of battles that followed the Parliamentarians gradually gained the upper hand, by the end of 1648 having control of the country with Charles as their prisoner. The King was now placed on trial as a 'tyrant, traitor, murderer and public enemy' and the death penalty passed upon him. On the 30th January 1649 the sentence was carried out with Charles being beheaded on a scaffold in front of Whitehall Palace. The monarchy was then declared to be at an end and a Commonwealth set up in its place.

In the battles and encounters of the Civil War Queenborough Castle had taken no direct part, remaining throughout in the undisputed hands of the Parliamentary forces. The Constable of the castle, Philip Herbert, Earl of Pembroke, who

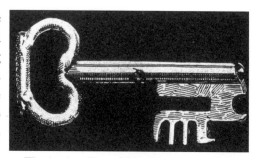

The Ancient Key of Queenborough Castle

44.

during the conflict had steadfastly espoused the Parliamentary cause, died while in London on the 23rd January 1650 and was buried in Salisbury Cathedral. He was to prove to be the last Custodian of Queenborough Castle for the year of his death was sadly also fated to be the year of the destruction of the castle. The Parliamentarians who, since the beginning of the Civil War, had held control of Queenborough, were practical men with little respect for tradition or history. Queenborough, as a royal castle, was officially seized by Parliament by an Ordnance of the 16th July 1648 and placed in the hands of a group of trustees who were to let it 'forthwith be surveycd and sold to supply the necessity of the State.' Parliament had decided to dispose of the castle in order to raise funds for the continuance of its cause. In the short term the castle was to be put to use for the incarceration of Royalist prisoners. At a meeting of the Council of State on the 6th August 1649 Queenborough Castle and Ostenhanger House were earmarked to be utilised as prisons for 'delinquents', provision to be made for the conducting of the prisoners to the castle and their upkeep while there.

By the time the required survey was completed the Civil War was over, the King was dead, and the Commonwealth under Oliver Cromwell established. The surveyors' report, finished and returned in 1650, gave a detailed account of the castle, which it described as being 'a capital messuage, called Queenborough Castle lyinge within the Common, belonginge to the Town of Queenborough, called Queenborough Marsh, in the parish of Minster, consisting about twelve rooms of one range of buildings below, and of about forty rooms from the first story upwards, beinge circular built with stone with six towers and certeine out offices thereunto belonginge, all the roofe thereof beinge covered with leade, whithin which circumference of the aforesaid castle is one little round court paved with stone, in the middle whereof one great well, and without which said castle one great court sirroundinge the said castle, which said court and castle beinge alsoe sirrounded with a greate stone wall, which said wall and castle beinge moated rounde in the outside thereof and abutting to the highway leading from the Town of Queenborough to Eastchurch, south, the whole coveringe three acres, one rood, and eleven perches of land.' The surveyors went on to report that 'the whole is much out of repair, and in noe way defensive to the Commonwealth being built in the tyme of bowes and arrowes, whereon noe plattforme can be erected for the plantinge of cannon, and it having noe command of the sea, although neare unto it' and concluded that 'it is not fit to be kept, but to be demolished,' finally estimating that the materials were worth, independently of the cost of taking it down, £1,792 12*s.* 0½*d.*

The reasons given for declaring the castle obsolete were almost certainly overstated. The castle had been much improved and well maintained by Sir Edward Hoby, and even total neglect by his successor, Philip Herbert, could not have brought about the state of advanced delapidation indicated in the report. Regarding the placement of guns, a fortress so sturdily built would be, with very little modification, more than capable of accommodating any of the cannon available during the Commonwealth period. The Parliamentarians had a natural prejudice against any Royal fortress but at the heart of their deliberations lay economic advantage; the castle was seen as a means by which to raise much needed funds. That the castle had 'no command of the sea' was the only comment in the survey to strike upon an undeniable truth. The real disadvantage of the castle had become its siting and, in this respect, doubts had long since grown as to its effectiveness. Over a century earlier, in 1547, Henry VIII had ordered that his fleet should be harboured in the Medway at 'Jillyngham Water' and, since this time, Chatham had become the chief base of the English navy. The mouth of the Medway was therefore placed in need of major protection against a surprise attack up the river by enemy ships. Because Queenborough lay to the south

Queenborough Castle During its Final Years
A Painting by Harold Batzer

of the point where Sheppey faced the Medway any ship entering the river lay well beyond the range of the castle's guns. The small blockhouse built by Henry at Sheerness was so placed that the river mouth was within the range of its cannon and, whenever peril threatened, it was kept at the ready to bombard any hostile vessels that might try to sail in. Garrisoned and maintained by the castle at Queenborough the blockhouse was a tangible reminder of the castle's own inadequacies in providing the required defence. In 1551 a new bulwark of greater strength was ordered to be erected at Sheerness and, in 1574, William Wynter, Surveyor of the Navy, and William Pelham, Lieutenant of Ordnance, were directed to provide timber and other materials, and to impress artificers and labourers for the erection of a small fort there. With the threat of a Spanish attack continuing to grow, in 1579, John Hawkins enlarged and reconstructed the fort on orders from the Privy Council, which likewise empowered him to impresss materials and men for the purpose. So it was that, by 1650, the development of the Medway as a navy base, and the consequent need to defend the river, had given cause for Sheerness rather than Queenborough to be regarded as having the greatest strategic importance on Sheppey. Some years later the view was to be upheld when, in 1667, a Dutch squadron broke into the Medway to decimate the fleet at Chatham and there was nothing a castle at Queenborough could have done to avert the disaster. The report of the Parliamentary surveyors was acted upon without delay, plans for a systematic demolition of the main body of the castle being got underway with, on the 17th July 1650, the materials sold off to a contractor, John Wilkinson, for the price named in the survey.

A few of the buildings standing within the castle grounds were, because they remained of commercial value, not destroyed but sold off:

> 'Know all men by thees pres'ts, that I, Daniel Judd of London, merchantt, have received and had att the sealing hereof, off Henry Segar of Quinburrowe in the county of Kent, Maior of the same, the sum of thirty pounds of lawful money of England, and is in full payment of and for that Barne, Stable, and Coach-house, wth th' app'tenanses, scituate and being w'thin the walls of Quinburrowe Castle aforesaid, and late belonging to the same Castle; and of and for all and eu'y the tymb's, stone, brick, tyles, and oth's the materialls thereto now belonging; and of and for all my whole right, tytle, and interest of, in, and to the same pr'mises and eu'y p't hereof; Off the w'h said su'me of xxx. soe by me received as aforesaid, I doe

cleerely acquitt and discharge the said Henry Segar, his eyers, adm's and assigneis, and eu'y of them for eu'r by theis pres'ts, sealled with my seale, dated the sixt day of Decemb'r No., 1650.

DANIELL' JUDD.

Sealled and d'd in the pres'nce of
Ralph Smith, John Wright.'

Oliver Cromwell
Lord Protector During the
Demolition of the Castle

Ralph Smith, 'Citizen and Skynner of London' who witnessed the above document, was the owner of half a dozen hoys small coastal trading vessels. He would now find lucrative long-term employment for his little fleet, plying between Queenborough and London to carry off the substantial quantities of stone being generated as the castle was dismantled. In London the unloaded stone was being put to use by the government in paving the streets around Whitehall. To facilitate the removal of the stone he had erected a wharf and cut a 'gripe' or small channel adjacent to the creek and castle. On the 22nd October 1651 he entered into an agreement with the town:

'That the said Ralph Smythe and his Assignes shall have the use of the wharfe which he hath nowe made neere the Castle at Queenborrough aforesaid and the way thereunto belonging during such tyme as he the said Ralph shall make use thereof and then to take away the said wharfe yf he please.

Itm. That the said Ralph Smyth shall have leave and libertie to enlarge the Gripe which he hath nowe made provided that it be noe way prejudiciall to the new Stables latelie built by Mr Henry Seagar.

Itm. That yf the said Ralph Smyth doe enlarge the Gripe then he shall make a sufficient carrying way at the North side of the Castle from the drawbridge to the way at the East side of the Castle and shall maintaine the same way for long as he makes use of the Gripe.

Itm. That yf the said Ralph Smyth shall not enlarge the Gripe then he shall make a sufficient Bridge or carrying way over the said Gripe and then the said Maior Jurats Bayliffe and Burgesses to maintaine the said Bridge and the carrying way att the South side of the Castle and the way at the North side of the Castle to[o] and not to be maintained by the said Ralph Smyth.

Itm. That the said Ralph Smyth and his Assigns shall pay unto the said Maior Jurats Bayliffe and Burgesses of Queenborrough aforesaid thirteen Shillings and fowre pence a yeare every yeare during such time and soe long as he or they shall make use of the said wharfe and the way thereunto belonging.

Itm. That the said Ralph Smyth shall lay all the stuffe that comes out of the Gripe uppon the Salts or in the Moate and shall not Annoy the Fresh lande therewith.'

Finding those manning his hoys being impressed into the Parliamentary navy Smith would deem it necessary on the 7th February 1654 to petition Oliver Cromwell, the Protector, for a licence to protect his crews from future seizure. He pointed out that although he had long supplied the State with paving stones he could now no longer do it, there being only one master and and crew member on each hoy, the rest of the men having been impressed. As a result of his petition Smith received, by order of the Protector, a warrant from the Council of State, dated 13th February 1654, giving the requested safeguards for his employees. Two years later, however, he was again obliged to petition Cromwell finding that his warrants to protect his ships and crews while conveying the stone to Whitehall, being of 'ancient' date, were no longer being obeyed. There was still a 'great want of stone' and in order to deliver it he needed fresh warrants. These were issued without delay by the Council on 15th February 1656. Exactly three years later, on 15th February 1659, he once again received protection, being granted a safe-pass for the six hoy masters to 'carry stores from Queenborough Castle to Whitehall for service of the State.'

The following year came the Restoration, bringing Charles II to the throne and an abrupt halt to the progressive demolition of Queenborough Castle that had been instigated by Parliament. By this time all that remained of the castle was a ruin. It then became the turn of successive generations of Islanders to further deplete the castle's structure, using the site as a convenient quarry whenever they needed building materials. Eventually all that could be usefully redeployed had been taken, and Queenborough Castle had

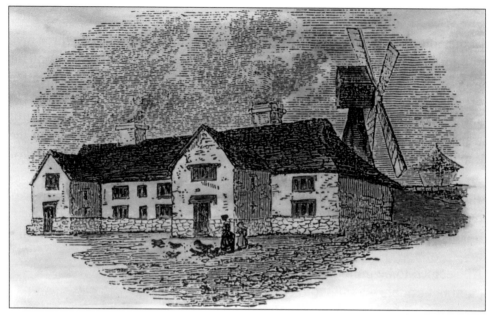

Local cottages built with materials removed from the castle ruins
A print from 1847 showing buildings long now demolished

effectively ceased to exist, only the castle well being preserved for the benefit of the town. Subsequent neglect by the Corporation to maintain the well in good order would result by the end of the seventeenth century in it yielding very little water and having fallen into disuse.

During the early part of the next century the want of fresh water at Sheerness Dockyard continued to be much felt and, except for collected rain-water, what was used was brought by water from Chatham. In an attempt to find a local supply, on 16th September of 1723 the 'Right Honourable the Navy Board' issued a warrant to the dockyard officers to survey the old well of the former castle at Queenborough. On Tuesday, the 24th September, the inspection of the well was made, no less than twelve of the officers being in attendance. They reported that they initially found very little water in the well. Having provided themselves with buckets and ropes a man was lowered down. He reported that the well was steined 200 feet down, with circular Portland stone, which was 'all entire, and stood fair.' The mean diameter was 4ft. 8 in., but wider above than below.

Finding that no water came in, preparations were made to bore deeper down, all details being recorded of how the work was subsequently carried out. On the 26th September, a baulk of timber some 7 feet long with a 3½-inch hole bored down its axis was been fixed vertically in rammed clay at the centre

50.

of the bottom of the well. A brick platform was built over this, then three men commenced boring with a 2½-inch augur. For three and a half days the augur was worked through a 'very close blueish clay,' but no water came. On the evening of the 30th 'the augur slipped down at once, and up came water.' In an hour the water was four feet deep, and in ten days there was 176 feet of water in the well. The distance bored was 81 feet, and they calculated the depth at which the water was found to be 166 feet below the deepest part of the adjacent sea. The quality of the water proved 'excellent, good soft, sweet, and fine.' They compared it with spring-water from Milton on the nearby mainland, and found it the better of the two. They 'put some soape to it, and it lathered finely.' They 'boiled old (*sic*) peas in it, which it performed well.'

The Ancient Queenborough Corporation Seal
Bearing a representation of the Castle's Main Gateway and Keep

All seemed to be going well at this point but trouble was about to erupt between the dockyard men and the townspeople. The former, in the belief that the castle site was Crown property, thought that they had full power to do as they pleased there without reference to the borough. The mayor and burgesses, on the other hand, viewed with growing outrage all the sudden activity around the well without them being consulted. Although through their bad management they had allowed the well to become defunct, they strongly objected to the idea of the navy now reopening the well and gaining exclusive access to the water. In their view the castle grounds, along with the well, had passed into the possession of the town at the time of the demolition of the castle.

All continued to go smoothly at the well until the next Friday morning. Mr. Bourne, the Foreman of Sheerness Dockyard, was engaged, it seems, in determining the best way of laying a lead pipe to conduct the water from the well to the banks of the nearby creek where the navy boats from Sheerness could fill their water casks. He had proceeded in making a plan of the castle land, and to measure the distance thence to the 'common creek that runs up at the back of the town,' where there had formerly been a wharf and small redoubt. Mr. Bourne was also intending to measure the distance to 'a very good wharf at the Copperas House.' However, then the townspeople reacted. 'Mr. Smith, the mayor, Mr. Iles, Mr. Evans, and Mr. John Jenkins, all of the Bench,' forbade this measurement to be made, but they, on being reasoned with, relented and went with Mr. Bourne, even assisting. Just then one Captain Evans came along, and persuaded the Mayor and the others not to 'give up the thing.' Mayor Smith, it appears, claimed a right to the castle and all appertaining thereto, and demanded the key of the well, threatening if it was not given to break the well open. This the dockyard officers refused to give up, but went peaceably away, merely setting a watch on the well.

Thus the matter stood, the officers claiming the King's right to the castle, land and well, and the corporation denying it. The Lords of the Treasury then sent a letter to the mayor and jurats on the 15th October notifying them that an official complaint had been received from the Navy Board concerning the town's obstructive attitude. The town countered on the 6th November, complaining of the navy's trespass on their property and asking that no approval should be given 'for conducting the water through the land belonging to the corporation or for debarring them the free use of it. The stand-off continued. Estimates were sent to the Navy Board of the cost of conveying the water from the castle well to the creek, but no work was initiated at Queenborough, and the navy began to consider alternative sources of water, test drillings being made in the Mote Marsh (Well Marsh) at Sheerness.

Eventually, in order to break the impasse over the well, the Navy Board decided upon a solution by which the town should be granted possession of

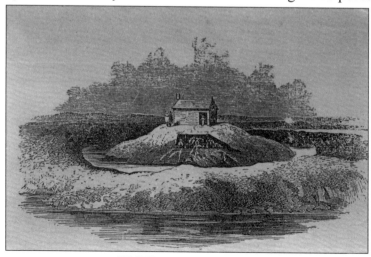

Well Hut on the Castle Site
From a Print Published in 1847

the well, while the same accepted that it was Crown property. In August 1725 the Board sent its representative, Mr. Scrope, down to Queenborough in order to deliver the well into the hands of the mayor and corporation. When, however, he approached 'Mr Evans (the father of the Mayor), who acts as his deputy, to deliver up to the Mayor and Corporation the care and inspection of the well of the Castle, and tendered a short instrument to him for the preservation of his Majesty's right in the well. He [Evans] replied that he would take care of the well; but treated the instrument with contempt, saying (with some warmth) that the seal of the Corporation should not be put to any such thing, insinuating that his Maty. had no right thereto.' Some more negotiations had then afterwards to take place before the well was placed at the disposal of the town, though it would still remain the property of the Crown, with the Commissioners of the Navy responsible for its maintenance.

The well was subsequently enclosed within a small hut-like structure with a pitched roof to protect the townspeople from the elements while they were winching up their buckets of water. In September 1817 a girl, having wound up the bucket of water, by accident suddenly let go of the winch handle. The handle, spinning round, struck a small child that was standing by, 'and dashing its brains out, killed it on the spot'.

In 1829 responsibility for the well was tranferred from the navy to the army. A letter of the 25th August to the mayor (Thomas Y. Greet) from Captain Robert Thomson, Officer Commanding the Royal Engineers at Sheerness, informed him that 'the Commissioners of the Victualling Department having delivered up the Well at Queenborough Castle to the Ordnance, I am directed by the Master General and Board, by their order dated 19th instant, to acquaint you therewith, and to give over the local Charge of the said well to the Corporation of Queenborough,' under the condition that 'the Corporation shall be at the Expense of its repairs and keep, until the Navy or Army may want a participation in its waters.'

In 1860 the Sittingbourne and Sheerness Railway Company opened its line, with the Railway Station for Queenborough placed on the eastern fringe of the castle site. Before the railway became operational the town passed the management of the well to the railway company. The water was required by the company as a convenient means of replenishing the tanks of its steam locomotives, no convenient water supply being available either at the Sheerness or Sittingbourne ends of the line. A small engine house was erected over the well, and a steam pump used to draw up the water which was then held in a large rectangular storage tank surmounting the roof of the building. The railway company, in return for being granted the use of its well undertook to pump up such water as was required for the use of the town free of charge, a boon to the inhabitants who instead of having to wind their water up could instead have it on tap.

When it was found necessary to increase the capacity of the pumping plant a 275 feet deep bore hole was also sunk about 25 feet to the northern side of the original well.

During the early years of the twentieth century the Rushenden Estate Company had constructed a water works on Rushenden Hill in order to supply its new housing development. In November 1905 negotiations were begun with Queenborough Town Council for supplying water to the borough. On recommendation of the Water Committee the Council purchased the works in the following year. Plans were formulated to increase the pumping capacity in order that a sufficient supply would be available for the whole town, with contracts being awarded to the constructors in May 1907. The enlargement work completed the town no longer required water supplied from the castle well which thenceforth was used exclusively for the needs of the railway company.

With the electrification of the railway line in 1959 the water was no longer required and the engine house was demolished, the castle mound being restored to the town for recreational purposes. The now redundant well was capped off but otherwise left intact, its position marked by a short vent pipe protruding from a slightly raised paved area at the centre of the site.

Queenborough Castle had represented a precious part of Sheppey's heritage, and its destruction constituted a sad and irreplaceable loss not only to historians but to all with an interest in the past. There is now little at Queenborough to indicate the former presence of the fortress. The eastern side of the site is still clipped by the main railway line to Sheerness and contains Queenborough Railway Station. A large Victorian school building, now used for other purposes, occupies part of the western edge of the site close to where there previously stood the main entrance to the castle. A small open green, rising slightly towards its centre, lies where once towered the majestic keep, a bricked and paved area covering the well, once the very centre of the castle. An information board erected by the council at the western side of the site gives visitors a brief description of the former castle.

INDEX